Nottingham's Trams & Trolleybuses

David J Ottewell

Nottinghamshire County Council
Community Services

Introduction

Trams and trolleybuses have played a significant role in the history of Nottingham over the last 100 years. Both arrived as innovations in the twentieth century and both, in their turn, have been superseded by other forms of public transport which their supporters claimed as more efficient and economical. It is a touch ironic that there are now plans to reintroduce trams to the City.

For the older reader, I hope the enclosed pictures and text stir memories of journeys around Nottingham, of places visited and people met.For the younger reader maybe a glance into a lost age.

As they used to say "Fares please! Hold yer Tight!" A journey around the Nottingham of the past is about to begin.

ISBN 0 902751 33 6

Contents

The conductor is boarding this trolleybus which is about to leave the Market Place on a journey to Trent Bridge via Arkwright Street. This six-wheeled vehicle was built in 1934.

A selection of trams around the Walter Fountain in Lister Gate. This fountain opened in July 1866 in memory of John Walter who represented Nottingham in Parliament. It had to be passed on either side by trams as it was sited in the centre of the road.

1. Early Days

The Nottingham and District Tramways Company Limited was formed in 1875 by a group of local businessmen. Two years later, in July 1877, they received Parliamentary permission to operate horse drawn trams in Nottingham directly competing with a number of horse drawn buses which ran around the town and to Carrington, St Ann's Well Road, Sneinton, Trent Bridge, Lenton and Basford.

The first two horse tram services began on Thursday 17th September 1878. Both commenced from St Peter's Church, one running via Carrington Street and Arkwright Street to Trent Bridge, the other to London Road via Carrington Street and Station Street. These routes were chosen to link Nottingham with its two main railway stations: the Midland Station on Station Street and the Great Northern on London Road. Eight single decker trams were purchased to operate these initial routes.

Horse drawn tramcar No. 10 outside the Town Arms, Trent Bridge c.1898-99.

A horse drawn tram making its way along London Road on the St. Peter's Church to London Road route, via Carrington Street and Station Street. This was a busy route linking the centre of Nottingham with the Great Northern railway station on London Road and the Midland Station on Station Street.

The following year, in August 1879, a service was introduced from the Market Place to Carrington and double decker cars joined the fleet. In June 1881 a line was opened to Basford which involved negotiating the steep 1:17 gradient of Derby Road. "Cock" or "Trace" horses were kept in Chapel Bar to help pull the trams up this steep incline. Other "Cock" horses were needed on Alfreton Road for the return journey.

Further extensions to the system followed in September 1881 with the Basford and Carrington services being linked by a track along Forest Road. This took the system to its maximum length of 7 miles and 40 chains.

Various types of trams were tried by the Company including, for a time, an experiment with a steam tram engine which operated to Isandulla Road in Basford.

In October 1897 Nottingham Corporation took up its option to buy the system at a cost of £80,000. Whilst they found the system in good condition, one of their first decisions was to paint the trams a uniform livery of maroon and cream. Prior to this each tram had been painted according to which route it operated. On acquiring the system the Corporation almost immediately looked to update the system by converting to overhead electrification.

2. Electric Trams Come to Nottingham

It was the Nottingham Corporation Act of 1899 which gave the Corporation powers to run an electric tramway system in Nottingham. Following an investigation of electric systems already in operation (including those as far away as New York and Boston) plans were drawn up and equipment ordered including a batch of 25 trams.

The first consignment of nine trams arrived in Nottingham in October 1900 and were taken to the depot at Sherwood for assembly. Meanwhile, track was laid from Sherwood along Mansfield Road into Nottingham and down Queen Street. A trial run was carried out by tram No. 4 on 17th November 1900, when instead of passengers, it was loaded with three tons of sand.

The service proper began on 1st January 1901. The two mile trip cost 2d and was immediately popular operating every five minutes with services being increased to every three minutes at peak times.

Open-topped tram No. 9. One of a batch purchased by the Corporation in 1900. It is seen here travelling away from the Market Place towards Chapel Bar.

Tram Sheds, Sherwood. It was from here on the morning of 1st January 1901 that Nottingham's first electric tram set out on its inaugural scheduled journey to the Market Place. The fare was 2d.

Open-topped tram No. 57 at the St Ann's Well Road terminus. This style of tram was not practical in Britain's variable weather and later all cars were fitted with tops. This conversion was carried out at the Corporation's Trent Bridge Works and cost £60 per vehicle.

Alfreton Road at the junction of Hartley Road and Bentinck Road. The box in front of the Board School provided shelter for boys who were employed to change the points at this junction on the tram network. The Lenton to Radford route (of which this junction was part) opened on 30th September 1902.

A 1905 postcard showing open-topped tram No. 43 passing the police station at Hyson Green.

Tram terminus at Bulwell. An early open-topped tram waits at the terminus before setting off on its journey to Trent Bridge via Nottingham Market Place.

New tramlines began to be laid in preparation for other services. The first of these commenced on 23rd July 1901 from Bulwell to Nottingham. The journey cost 3d. Replacement of the horse tramlines was also carried out so that the Sherwood service could be extended via Station Street to Trent Bridge and a separate Trent Bridge route could be run to the Market Place. This operated every three minutes apart from at peak times when a two minute service was provided. By the end of the first year 77 trams were being used to operate the network.

Further developments took place in 1902. On 21st February the St Ann's Well Road to the Market Place route opened with a service every five minutes, It was decided that the remaining horse tram routes were no longer viable and two of the remaining 13 horse trams were sold to Leicester Corporation for further use. The remaining 11, plus 60 horses and sundry other items, were sold for £1,335.

Market Place, Bulwell c.1904. The service from Bulwell began operation on 23rd July 1901 and closed on 12th May 1934.

Chapel Bar with an open-topped tram on the Bulwell to Trent Bridge route.

After passing the Walter Fountain trams such as Car No. 42, seen here, continued their journey along Carrington Street towards the Midland Station.

A little further along Carrington Street this tram is seen close to the James Store which was one of many shops in what was a thriving retail area in the earlier years of the Twentieth Century.

The tram terminus at Mapperley with a tram waiting for passengers. Trams were used as moving advertising hoardings with this one advertising locally produced Raleigh cycles.

On 13th May 1902 the Mapperley route was brought into operation with a service running every six minutes from Trent Bridge and alternating between the Mapperley terminus and Alexandra Park. This was quickly followed by the Nottingham Road to Station Street route which opened on 7th July.

Two further routes were introduced later in 1902 to meet increased demand. On 30th September the Lenton and Radford route opened; while on 8th November the Wilford Road service began. Initially, the latter linked with the St Ann's Well Road route to provide a through service but this practice was quickly discontinued. However, another two services were successfully linked into a single long route running from Bulwell to Trent Bridge. By the end of the second year of operation the Corporation had purchased a total of 105 trams.

Car No. 120, built in 1908, makes its way gingerly down Woodborough Road. The gradient on this road was 1:11·5, the steepest on the whole network.

A pair of trams on the Mapperley route about to pass each other on Woodborough Road.

3. The Tramway System Develops.

Only one new service commenced in 1903 when a section of track to Hartley Road was opened on 27th July. This linked with existing track on the St. Ann's Well Road and Nottingham Road routes forming a section known as the "Boulevard Circle".

At this time tram routes were not indicated by numbers, but carried destination boards on the front and sides. For those unable to read these also had their own colours. These were:-

Sherwood to Station Street - white on red.

Mapperley to Trent Bridge - blue on yellow

St. Ann's Well Road to Boulevards - green on white.

Nottingham Road to Boulevards - white on blue.

Wilford Road to Market Place - white on green.

Bulwell to Trent Bridge - red on white.

Basford to Market Place - white on black.

At night trams carried different coloured lights to inform passengers of their destination.

The St Ann's Well Road service began operation on 21st February 1902, continuing until February 1930.

St Ann's Well Road tram terminus. Before the tram routes were numbered in 1912 this service had white destination boards with green lettering. At night it carried green lights to identify its route.

Another tram on the St Ann's Well Road route. No. 37 was originally built as an open-topped tram in 1901 and later roofed.

An Edwardian view of a tram approaching the Oliver Cromwell pub in Commercial Square, St Ann's Well Road.

At the bottom of Parliament Street stood the familiar landmark of the Palais de Dance, opened in 1925. A route 6 tram passes by.

Car No. 57 travelling up Alfreton Road towards Canning Circus. Appropriately the front of the tram advertises Raleigh Cycles for it was in this area of Nottingham that the Company was founded by Frank Bowden.

Both Route 2 from Mapperley and Route 3 from Bulwell terminated at Trent Bridge. Notice the horse bus overtaking its mechanised rivals.

The electrified tramway system in Nottingham had grown rapidly in its first three years of operation and after the opening of the Hartley Road extension in 1903 the Corporation began a process of consolidation. No new routes were begun or new trams purchased for the next four years. The Corporation, however, was not idle. In 1903 it agreed to experiment with roofing the old open-topped trams. This adaptation initially cost £85 per vehicle but proved popular and resulted in increased passenger use. Further cars were similarly adapted, the cost being reduced to £60 per car, so that by 1909 seventy two of the 125 trams in service were covered. Other changes at this time included the fitting of more powerful engines to the older trams.

In 1906 the Corporation agreed to a change of positioning of the traction poles for the trams. Hitherto they had been sited in the middle of the road but this was found to impede traffic flow and from this time onward side poles were introduced.

The junction of King Street and Queen Street. The obelisk on the left is the Boer War memorial which was unveiled in 1903. The tram in the distance has just passed on a journey from Mapperley to Trent Bridge.

Trams at the Trent Bridge terminus, Route 2. They ran from here via the Market Place to Mapperley.

A busy Market Place scene with both covered and open-topped trams in evidence. Queen Victoria's statue stands in the foreground dominating the scene.

Compare this to the previous picture. Here the stalls have been removed from the Market Place. Note the multiplicity of tram lines.

The frustrated cry of "never a bus when you want one and then three come together" would appear to have applied equally to trams if this postcard view of Long Row is anything to go by. Half a dozen covered trams plus an earlier open-topped car are on view.

Car No. 38 on the Colwick Road route which operated from 14th March 1907 to 1st June 1935. An example of the ornate poles used to support the overhead wires may be clearly seen.

In 1907 the Corporation set out to further extend the tramway system in Nottingham. On the 14th March the Market Place to Colwick Road section opened and the following week this route was linked to the Basford service to form one long route. On the 15th March a route to Trent Bridge via London Road was inaugurated linking up with the Wilford Road service. These two new extensions necessitated the purchase of ten new trams in each of the next two years bringing the total to 125.

The next addition to the system came on 16th December 1910 when the Carlton Road Service began operation, initially extending from the Market Place to Thorneywood Lane (Porchester Road).

Colwick Road. The tram is stationary and the conductor has dismounted to pose for the photographer. In the background is the railway crossing.

A tram passing through Sneinton on Route 4. The picture clearly illustrates just how much of the road trams took up.

A bustling Sneinton Market with a tram in the distance near the Victoria Baths. The baths opened in 1850 when they were known as Gedling Street Baths and were re-named in 1896.

Parliament Street at its junction with Milton Street. A policeman stands in the middle of the road as a pair of trams approach.

The statue of Samuel Morley (a former M.P. and passionate advocate of libraries for children) looks down on passing tram No. 96. The destination board indicates Basford-Market Place-Colwick.

An innovation occurred in November 1912 when, instead of coloured destination boards, tram routes were allocated numbers.

The routes were:-

        1. Sherwood to Trent Bridge

        2. Mapperley to Trent Bridge

        3. Bulwell to Trent Bridge

        4. Basford to Colwick

        5. Nottingham Road to Radford and Lenton

        6. St Ann's Well Road to Radford and Lenton

        7. Wilford Road to London Road

        8. Carlton Road to Market Place.

To celebrate the Coronation of King George V and Queen Mary on 22nd June 1911 a tramcar was decorated and illuminated by hundreds of lights and was then run over various routes on the tramway system.

A busy scene at the junction of Parliament Street and Milton Street with trams operating on routes 4, 5 and 7 converging. Horse drawn vehicles and motor cars are also in view.

Carlton Tram Terminus. This section of the tramway system was opened on 10th December 1910 with an extension added on 14th June 1914.

A new wave of extensions to the system took place in 1914. On 1st January a new section of line was brought into operation running from Basford to Cinderhill. This linked with the existing tram route from Ripley operated by the Nottinghamshire and Derbyshire Tramway Company. The Carlton Road route was also extended, first with a new terminus on Standhill Road (opened on 5th January) and subsequently with a regular service to Carlton from 14th June.

The same year (1914) also saw work begin on the Derby Road route to Gregory Street which was opened on 25th September with a service every ten minutes. This became Route 9 with trams leaving the Market Place terminus via Market Street and arriving via Chapel Bar. Track was also laid from Sherwood out to Arnold with that service opening on 1st January 1915. It was linked to the Derby Road route and thus became part of Route 9 making it the longest route on the Nottingham system. An extra 20 trams were ordered to cope with the increased working, bringing the fleet up to 155.

Tram Cars No. 146 and No. 128 passing each other on Mansfield Road. Travelling towards them is a milkman with his horse and cart.

This tram, which has travelled into Nottingham from Sherwood, is approaching the Old Corner Pin pub on the corner of Clumber Street.

4. The First World War Years

The First World War frustrated further development of Nottingham's tramway system and plans for a proposed line to Beeston had to be shelved. Many of the Corporation's employees were called up for military service and, in October 1915, the first group of women were employed as tram conductresses. Hours of operation were reduced during wartime although the post-war era saw demand rise to greater heights: in 1920 an extra 25 trams were purchased. It was at this time too that the Corporation first introduced buses to supplement the tram services. The first service operated from Bentinck Road to Bagthorpe and proved popular with demands for further such services to be provided.

Nottingham's Midland Station, a prominent landmark on the journey from the city centre to the Trent Bridge terminus.

Lady Tram Conductor, Nottingham Corporation. Local company, C. and A. G. Lewis produced this postcard during the First World War. At this time a number of female conductors were introduced to replace men who had gone to fight in the War but this was always regarded as a temporary measure.

Derby Road, Lenton was the terminus for Route 9. A motorcycle and sidecar is just passing stationary tram No. 129.

A view from Parliament Street into Milton Street where a tram may be seen travelling on Route 1 towards Sherwood.

The corner of King Street and Market Place with tram No. 111 on the Sherwood route. The journey up to Parliament Street involved quite a steep climb. A strangely bedecked Exchange may be seen in the background.

Bulwell Market Place with tramcar No. 173 waiting to depart. A large gathering of locals is also posing for the photographer.

Between 1920 and 1925 no further trams were bought by the Corporation and no new routes introduced. During this time, however, the Corporation purchased 35 motor buses to extend that part of its services and in 1925 was successful in an application to Parliament for permission to operate trolleybus services in Nottingham. Could this be signalling the beginning of the end of trams in Nottingham?

Another phase of tramway development took place in 1926 when on 7th June a new tramway extension was opened from Woodborough Road to Westdale Lane. The Corporation also invested in 20 new trams bringing the fleet total to 200. The tramway system in Nottingham was now at its greatest extent, totalling 25·9 miles.

Tram No. 165 travelling along Vernon Road, Basford, on its way to the terminus at Bulwell. Note the unusual three-wheeled vehicle parked outside the shops.

Derby Road provided a steep thoroughfare into and out of the centre of Nottingham. This tram, on Route 3, is destined for Trent Bridge.

A pair of trams has just passed on a busy Arkwright Street. Car No. 196, one of the last to be purchased by the Corporation, is closest to the camera.

Arkwright Street. The tram on Route 3 is close to one of the 12 steel bridges which, along with over 50 stone arches, carried the Great Central railway line from the Trent to Victoria Station.

5. The Tramway System Declines

From 1927 the tramway system in Nottingham began a slow decline. A trolleybus service had commenced on 10th April of that year on the Nottingham Road route and the trams were withdrawn. A week later (16th April) a short extension was made to the tram system with trams being able to run from Gregory Street, Lenton to Wollaton Park gates.

Between 1926 and 1929 redevelopment work took place in the centre of Nottingham around the Market Place. This included the removal of the traditional market and the demolition of the Exchange to be replaced by today's Council House. Because of these changes the tramlines also had to be altered. Apart from this spending, investment in the tramway system was severely limited with money being diverted towards motor bus and trolleybus services.

Looking from the Council House which opened in 1929. A pair of trams wait beside the newly laid out Market Square. While redevelopment work was being undertaken, the opportunity was seized to move some of the tram lines closer to the side of the road.

Parliament Street showing a tram on Route 4. Note the Theatre Royal (right) and the Hippodrome Theatre in the background.

In 1930 Parliament passed the Nottingham Corporation Bill effectively allowing the remaining tram services in Nottingham to be replaced by trolleybuses. The tram routes to Wilford Road and St Ann's Well Road were discontinued and the number of trolleybuses owned by the Corporation rose to 24. The bus fleet meanwhile increased to 103.

The following year (29th November 1931) a circular trolleybus route was introduced to replace the Derby Road tram route. This was followed on 19th March 1932 by trolleybuses taking over from trams on the Carlton Road route. The number of trams in service was reduced to 158.

Theatre Square with the Theatre Royal in the background. Tram No. 67 is en route to Radford. It is about to be overtaken by an enthusiastic motorcyclist. Note the once familiar Player's Navy Cut advert beside the theatre.

The key development in 1933, apart from trolleybuses replacing trams on the Basford to Cinderhill extension, was the changing of the tram route numbers to letters. The purpose of this was to avoid confusion with the new trolleybus services. The following year, meanwhile, saw even greater activity in the conversion programme: tram numbers in the fleet were reduced to 83 and on 12th May the last trams ran on the Bulwell, Trent Bridge and Lenton and Radford routes. The Colwick Road and London Road sections were closed in 1935 and the fleet was reduced to 40 trams. Six of the surplus vehicles found their way to Buenos Aires in Argentina.

Old meets new as tramcar No. 49 (Route 7) built in 1901, meets No. 182 (Route 3) one of the last batch of twenty cars purchased in 1926. These were sold after the system was closed in 1936 and went on to operate in Aberdeen.

Route 6 at the junction of Lenton Boulevard and Derby Road. The tram is prominently advertising Campion Cycles which were manufactured in Nottingham at the beginning of the Twentieth Century.

6. The Ripley Rattler

The Notts. And Derbyshire Tramway Company's trams which ran from Ripley to Nottingham are included in this book because this system linked with the Nottingham tramway at Cinderhill. The Notts. And Derbyshire trams used Nottingham Corporation's lines to run from the edge of the city to a terminus on Upper Parliament Street (outside what is now the Nottingham Co-operative Society building).

This route is claimed to have been the most dangerous in the British Isles owing to its length and the gradients involved: from Cinderhill to Ripley there was only a single track system with 316 passing loops.

A limited service commenced on 4th July 1913 while the full route became operational on 1st January 1914. The last tram ran on 5th October 1932. It quickly obtained the nickname "The Ripley Rattler".

A "Ripley Rattler" in Upper Parliament Street waiting to begin the 15 mile trip to Ripley. The journey took one hour 40 minutes.

Main Street, Kimberley. The first 12 trams purchased by the Notts. and Derbyshire Company were of the open-topped variety like this one. They had seating for 32 on the upper deck and 24 in the relative comfort of the saloon.

Nottingham Road, Eastwood. Another 12 trams with covered tops were later bought. The colouring was light green and cream with gold lining.

7. The System Closes Down

1936 was a very important year in the history of public transport in Nottingham. The undertaking changed its name from the Nottingham Corporation Passenger Transport Department to Nottingham City Transport. Mapperley trams ceased operation on 1st February and, on 5th September 1936, the last ever tram service in Nottingham was run over the Arnold route. The final tram No. 190 was driven into the Parliament Street depot, after its historic last journey, by the Chairman of the Transport Committee, Alderman J. Farr J.P.

Tram No. 182 seen outside Victoria Station on the final day of tram services in Nottingham. The trams' replacements - buses and trolleybuses - were already in service as can be seen to the right of this picture near the Victoria Hotel.

The last tram services in Nottingham operated to Arnold. Here tramcar No. 97 can be seen travelling near the Arnold terminus.

The Bonington Theatre, Arnold c.1932-35. Car No. 181 was one of the last to be bought by the Corporation. After the closure of the Nottingham System, in September 1936, this vehicle saw further service in Aberdeen.

8. Birth of the Trolleybus Era

As early as 1908 the trackless vehicles then coming to prominence in Europe were being kept under review by Nottingham Corporation with a view to introducing a similar system in Nottingham. In 1913 plans were drawn up for a trolleybus route from the Market Place via Arkwright Street to Trent Bridge. Although permission was granted the scheme did not progress as the First World War frustrated any plans for alteration and expansion.

On 10th January 1924 the Corporation sent a delegation to inspect the Birmingham trolleybus system. Favourable reports were received and the Government were asked for permission to convert the tram routes along Nottingham Road, Wilford Road and Wells Road to trolleybus working. This was granted with the proviso that the new vehicles weighed less than nine tons gross.

Trolleybus No. 10 pictured turning onto Mansfield Road in April 1932. Although given the number 10 in the fleet, this vehicle was the first to be delivered to Nottingham ready for the opening of the service in April 1927. It had originally been on show at the 1925 Olympia Exhibition and came to Nottingham prior to the other trolleybuses in the first order so that drivers and conductors could be trained before the service commenced.

An early trolleybus at the junction of Mansfield Road and Gregory Boulevard. Route 37 ran from King Street to Haydn Road via Nottingham Road. The building in the background is the old Carrington Railway Station.

To set up the Nottingham trolleybus system the Corporation ordered ten vehicles from Railless Ltd. of Rochester, Kent. Their delivery was held up by the General Strike of 1926, but eventually they arrived and trials and training began. The first vehicle ran from the King Street, Queen Street junction via Parliament Street, Milton Street, Mansfield Road, Sherwood Rise to Nottingham Road. It carried Route No. 5 like the tram it replaced.

In spite of the extensive plans initially put to Parliament Route 5 was the only trolleybus service introduced into Nottingham for over three years. The popularity and versatility of the new "trackless" vehicles soon led to the Corporation trying to add to the fleet and convert more routes but problems were encountered; not least that Railless had decided to stop making trolleybuses. A different company, Ransome, Sims and Jeffries of Ipswich were given the order and their vehicles included such modifications as pneumatic tyres which were lacking on the first trolleybuses.

9. Inter-War Expansion

Expansion of the trolleybus system proceeded slowly. Trial vehicles were borrowed from other places such as Wolverhampton and Doncaster and council officials visited systems already in operation in Maidstone, Doncaster and Wolverhampton. Eventually on 20th March 1930 the long-standing plans to operate trolleybuses along Wilford Road and Wells Road came to fruition.

The Nottingham Corporation Bill of 1930 proposed replacing all existing tram routes with trolleybuses and introducing many new extensions. While the House of Commons gave the ideas their blessing, the House of Lords were more circumspect and refused permission for any new routes outside the City boundary. At this time the trolleybus fleet consisted of 24 vehicles but the Company demonstrated their commitment to trolleybus services by placing orders for 25 new vehicles.

By 1930 there were 24 trolleybuses in operation in Nottingham along with 200 trams and 103 motor buses. This "trackless" registration number TV754 was No. 24 in the fleet and is seen travelling on the Wilford Road route negotiating the turn from Parliament Street into George Street.

TV 744 was built by Ransome, Sims and Jeffries in 1930 and was one of the first trolleybuses in Nottingham to have six wheels. This photograph, taken in August 1933, shows it travelling down Mansfield Road towards Victoria Station. Note the street furniture.

Trolleybus No. 22 bedecked with an advert "Drink Apollo". This vehicle is pictured on Wilford Road en route to Wells Road.

Roadworks on Parliament Street outside the Milton's Head Hotel in March 1934 did not stop the flow of trolleybuses, although the poles appear stretched to their limit as No. 23 follows a course along the tram lines closely pursued by a pair of trams.

It was not always a straightforward matter to replace tram routes with trolleybuses. Trolleybuses needed turning points, which for instance, produced a delay in running trolleybuses into Carlton until demolition work could take place in Post Office Square. This service finally opened on 29th November 1930. The same day also saw the commencement of a circular service to Wollaton Park with its Nottingham terminus at the Central Market. The following year these two routes were amalgamated.

A damp September day in 1935 but there is still lots of activity as trolleybus No. 39, built by Ransomes, using a body manufactured by Brush of Loughborough, approaches Victoria Station. At this stage the trolley wires were widely spaced. Later it was standard practice to set them closer together. To the left is the old Regent Cinema.

A trolleybus being delivered for use on the Nottingham system. This vehicle was constructed in 1934 using a chassis supplied by Ransome, Sims and Jeffries and a body from the Brush works in Loughborough.

Lack of funds prevented further expansion in 1932 and 1933, although the Corporation still managed to convert the Cinderhill section of tramway to trolleybus working. This was important because it allowed the Notts. and Derbyshire. Traction Company to begin operating over the route from Ripley to Nottingham with trolleybuses which they had introduced to replace the "Ripley Rattler" tram.

On the 13th May 1934 the Bulwell and Arkwright Street routes were converted to trolleybuses and an extension was built to the Bulwell Hall Estate. By this time the Nottingham trolleybus fleet numbered 106, making it the largest in England. The conversion lost some of its momentum at this point as the very pro-trolleybus General Manager, Mr W G Marks left to be replaced by the less sympathetic Mr J L Gunn.

The tram route to Bulwell was converted to trolleybus running in May 1934, the same month as this photograph was taken. Trolleybus No. 80, recently purchased to operate on the new route, waits to depart with the premises of Hope Bros. and Griffin and Spalding in the background.

A line of trolleybuses inside the depot. At the front is No. 107 which was one of a group of 30 Leyland buses purchased in 1935. Unusually for pre-war trolleys they had all metal bodies and were the first trolleybuses to be fitted with large destination screens.

On May 12th 1937 the Corporation decorated a trolleybus and a motor bus to celebrate the Coronation of King George VI and Queen Elizabeth. This picture shows the trolleybus: the motor bus was decorated as a replica of Nottingham Castle. Both vehicles made runs over various routes on Coronation Day.

By 1938 the Nottingham trolleybus system was so well regarded around the world that delegations came from as far afield as Belfast and Bergen in Norway to see how it operated. In Nottingham, however, people were already beginning to have doubts about the future of trolleybuses especially with the rise in price of electricity. Thoughts turned to replacing the "trackless" with motor buses as had already happened in nearby Chesterfield.

10. Wartime Operation

The start of the Second World War in September 1939 resulted in a number of changes to the trolleybus service in Nottingham. Vehicles had their side and rear windows painted over and in some cases blinds attached to aid the blackout. Interior lights were screened and adaptations made to reduce sparks on overhead wires. Motorists and passengers were aided with changes made to the trolleybus livery with white wings and platform edges added.

The war took away a number of employees and women were once again called into service as conductresses. By 1942 there was also a shortage of drivers and in July of that year the first woman trolleybus driver took to the road. By October 1944 a total of 25 female trolleybus drivers were employed.

Route 39 began on Middleton Boulevard at Wollaton and entered Nottingham via Ilkeston Road. The trolleybus would then travel down Parliament Street on its way to Post Office Square, Carlton. This photograph was taken in May 1940 and clearly shows how the word "Nottingham" in front of City Transport has been painted out. This was a wartime precaution intended to confuse the enemy in the event of a sudden invasion.

Another trolleybus photographed in 1940. The Second World War resulted in a number of changes to trolleybuses and their operation. Hours were restricted, women were employed, blinds were used to cover windows and, as seen here, vehicle edges were painted white so as to be more clearly visible at ground level in the blackout.

When the tram system was finally discontinued in 1936 trolleybuses were free to ply their trade up and down Arkwright Street providing an efficient service between Trent Bridge and the centre of Nottingham.

A large queue waits to board trolleybus No. 128 at the Nottingham Terminus for Bulwell. This photograph was taken in August 1935 when No. 128 was new to the fleet. It had a Leyland chassis with an all metal Metro-Cammell body.

Trolleybus No. 140 standing outside the now demolished Victoria Station. This vehicle began life with Cleethorpes Corporation in 1938. When war broke out in 1939 new buses proved difficult to acquire and four trolleybuses had to be bought second hand from Cleethorpes and repainted in Nottingham colours. This picture dates from August 1949.

The demand for trolleybus services continued, and indeed increased, during wartime. The lack of new vehicles meant the Corporation had to look for other sources of vehicles. Seaside resorts reduced their services because of the war so Nottingham bought trolleybuses from Southend on Sea and Cleethorpes. The need for more vehicles became so great that in 1941 six single decker trolleybuses, with only limited accommodation, were purchased from the Hastings Tramways Company. These were quickly nicknamed "kiddy cars" by the public.

On the evening of 8th May 1941 Nottingham was hit by a severe air raid. The windows of ten trolleybuses were smashed and a number of overhead wires brought down. Services, however, were not disrupted for long.

In 1942 five trolleybuses originally destined for South Africa were acquired for Nottingham. They were unusual in that they were eight feet wide which was six inches wider than normal. The supply situation began to improve and in 1943 Nottingham received an allocation for four of the new wartime standard design trolleybuses. These were supplemented by a further seven in the following year.

Trolleybus No. 357, built in 1934 by Karrier, is parked on Middleton Boulevard in March 1940. It shows wartime adaptations to lights, trolley leads and paint work. Note the contraption on the side of the road near where the driver is standing. During the war these were set up all over Nottingham and in the event of an air raid they could be lit resulting in dense smoke to form a protective smokescreen.

The trolleybus to the right has a destination board indicating Ripley. These vehicles were a familiar sight in Nottingham after 1933 when they were introduced to replace the "Ripley Rattler". The service continued until 25th April 1953. Both trolleybuses are poised to make the sharp turn from King Street into Queen Street.

11. A Last Flourish

With the return of peace in 1945 there was once again talk of abandoning the trolleybus system in Nottingham, but no action was taken immediately. Indeed a new service, with the number 48, was introduced running from Nottingham Road to Trent Bridge, and in early 1946 ten new trolleybuses were delivered.

The first post-war designed trolleybuses arrived in Nottingham late 1948, but it was the 1949 delivery of the larger capacity (70 seater) 30 feet long, 8 feet wide vehicles that became the most significant development. These, along with some 7ft 6ins wide trolleybuses delivered in 1950, totalled 30 vehicles which meant that much needed updating of the fleet could begin. The larger vehicles were liked by many, leading to a substantial repeat order totalling 67 vehicles. By the end of 1952 these had all arrived, allowing all the remaining pre-war vehicles to be removed from service, leaving a fleet of 155.

Trolleybus No. 523 on Parliament Street with passengers boarding in order to travel along the route towards Post Office Square, Carlton. This vehicle was one of the extra large 1949-50 batch which operated from the nearby Parliament Street depot.

KTV 506 was built in 1949-50. It was one of a delivery of 25 trolleybuses, the first new six-wheelers since before the Second World War. They had metal bodies and were in the new larger size of 30 feet long and 8 feet wide. They proved a good purchase as most remained in service until the last days of the trolleys.

An unusual single deck trolleybus operated by Nottingham City Transport for a short while in 1953 in an effort to reduce costs. Loaned from Glasgow Corporation it had a rear entrance and central exit. There was seating for 27 while a further 27 could be accommodated standing up. The conductor sat at a cash desk near the door taking fares. Unfortunately the strange door positions caused difficulties for passengers boarding and alighting especially at stops with shelters and the experiment was abandoned.

Theatre Square with the Gaumont Cinema and the County Hotel in the background. A trolleybus is about to pass the old AA offices on its way down Parliament Street.

Another of the 1949-50 batch of larger six-wheeled trolleybuses. This one is making light work of the wintry conditions as it travels from Theatre Square along Parliament Street on Route 39 to Carlton.

Trolleybus No. 575 at the entrance to the Embankment. This trolley was built in 1951-52 by which time it had been decided to revert to 7ft 6ins trolleybuses as these could operate throughout the system without restriction.

The last group of trolleybuses were acquired by Nottingham Corporation in 1951-52 and were numbered to 601. This vehicle No. 598, photographed at Cinderhill, is from that final select delivery. It is operating on Route 41 which extended from King Street, Nottingham to Bells Lane at Cinderhill.

12. The End of the Trolleybuses

After a rush of activity at the beginning of the 1950's trolleybuses seemed to go out of fashion in Nottingham. No new vehicles were bought and by 1960 fifteen trolleybuses had been taken out of service, their place being taken by motor buses where necessary.

The first trolleybus route to be completely changed to motor bus operation was Route 45 from Wollaton Park to Trent Bridge. This had begun operation in 1935 and had always carried fewer passengers than other routes. The change took place on 4th November 1962.

Plans were made to convert other routes and when the change came it arrived suddenly. Between April and October 1965 Routes 43, 41, 39, 40 and 47 were all transferred to motor bus operation. Most trolleybuses were decommissioned as being surplus to requirements with only about a dozen being needed to run the skeleton service which remained.

Ironically, the last route to continue trolleybus operation was the one that had started it all way back in 1927: from King Street - Queen Street to Nottingham Road. This finally ceased operation on 30th June 1966. To round off the era of trolleybuses in Nottingham a special commemorative trip was arranged in a repainted trolleybus on the 1st July 1966. The era of the "trackless", fondly remembered by many of the older citizens of Nottingham, was finally over.

Trolleybus No. 520 parked on Nottingham Road, Basford on 30th June 1966. Note the dent in the rear wing and the scratches down the side. Since it was the last day of service it was probably thought too late to effect cosmetic repairs.

The last trolleybus route to be operated in Nottingham was Queen Street to Nottingham Road, Basford. This saw its final service on 30th June 1966.

As a celebration of the trolleybuses in Nottingham vehicle No. 506, which had been built in 1949-50, was given a special livery and a commemorative trip was run on 1st July 1966.